THE CHI BOOK:

Reiki from the Roots

by

Sarah Luczaj

W

Cover design Spanky Pymm

British Library Cataloguing-in-Publication Data

ISBN 978-1-913140-26-7 in epub format

ISBN 978-1-913140-27-4 in mobi format

ISBN 978-1-913140-28-1 in azw3 format

ISBN 978-1-913140-29-8 in pdf format

ISBN 978-1-913140-30-4 in print format

Part micro-memoir, part user's guide to the primordial power of the universe, THE CHI BOOK: Reiki from the Roots, vibrates with raw energy and calms like still water. It sings us awake from our collective illusion of powerlessness. It is a path, lit with the specific flavor of Dr. Sarah Luczaj's direct experience and studied expertise.

I know I will return to it again and again. For solace. For illumination. For wisdom.

Kim Noriega, Poet/ Teacher
www.kimnoriega.com

This book starts off as an introductory walk with a Master into the formless art and energy through the form of her beautiful, true, and sometimes funny words and resonant paragraphs. Even as a Reiki Master myself, I was learning from this book.

Carolina Isabel Rodriguez, Reiki Master
www.thecarolinaisabel.com

What you are holding in your hands is a living transmission of Reiki, of the Tao. It is a shimmering glimpse into the infinite possibilities of the Great Mystery & an invitation to welcome this energy into your unique web of life. Sarah herself is an activation & emanation of Reiki. This book is sure to awaken deep inner gnosis & illuminate your Reiki path.

Never before have I found such a poetic tapestry of this ancient healing art.

Adrianna Velez Reiki Master/Teacher, Alchemical life coach
www.sweetmedicina.com

Sarah Luczaj is a person centred counsellor who worked in private practice in rural Poland for almost two decades, and is now based in Glasgow. She runs live and online workshops in the Creative Regeneration process, which involves a specific blend of focusing, meditation, free-writing and intuitive painting. The Creative Regeneration process links and crystallises her own Buddhist and focusing practices as well as her experience and skills as a poet, writer and literary translator who is also actively involved in visual art and music.

Sarah is also the co-founder of the terrealuma healing refuge (www.terrealuma.com), a centre for spiritual activism and creative bliss, in Poland. The refuge aims to facilitate healing through reconnection to nature, on all levels from the nutritional, through permaculture practices and use of wild herbs, to the creative and spiritual. She is also a Reiki practitioner (at Master level), staying close to the original roots of Reiki in Buddhist and Taoist practices.

She is the author of 'An Urgent Request' (2009, Fortunate Daughter Press) and Creative Regeneration (2019 Wayward Publications Ltd).

Contents

RADICAL CHI MANIFESTO

The storm blows
on the world, don't be moved
human heart,
root like a pine tree
on a rock

(09 Emporer Meiju, Waka poem, my translation from Rivard, R 2007)

Chi is life energy.

Literally.

It's the energy which makes the difference between a person, animal or plant being alive, and being dead.

Chi is not something apart from what we are.

Chi can't be owned, given or taken away.

It isn't information, it can't be taught. It has its own intelligence.

Left to its own devices, it is in the nature of chi to flow. The flow of chi is quintessentially natural. It's possible, however, to partially block or interfere with the flow.

Then, skills are involved in creating proper conditions so it may move unimpeded, exactly as it is.

The brains of many, if not most, people on the planet are now constantly bathed in some form of electromagnetic frequency — quite a fresh occurrence in human history. People carry devices around like life-support machines as if to keep their brainwaves constantly attuned to those frequencies — frequencies of dissociation and scatteredness, of constant checking and constant reacting, rather than creating. Of addictive pseudo-action on the mental plane alone.

This maintains fear and anxiety as a constant state. Fear and anxiety held in the system, maintained permanently, create a sense of helplessness that leaves you open to exploitation, and uses up precious resources in your nervous system, leaving you depleted.

If you live in accordance with the natural flow of the chi, there's no holding on to fear. Fear's just a response to situations, which appears when necessary then goes away again. If the chi is not fully flowing, and a situation perceived to be life-threatening happens — you can't react. That's when trauma sets in.

You dissociate, split the life-threatening experience off from your memory, go dead to your own experience. This is all too common, it even seems normal.

So, in the present day context, with disconnection and trauma rife and institutionalised, with people making money from keeping your energy scattered, the function of Reiki or healing-with-the-chi gains a new twist. All the ancient traditions of energy healing — different ways of amplifying and transmitting the chi - are needed as never before. Reiki is one of them, and a simple one to grasp.

The world needs chi warriors now. Not to fight on one side versus the other, but to stand up and fight for what is all-encompassing, generative and primordial. Not just because we all deserve better than this, but because the linear logic of capitalism, of endless growth, accumulation and consumption and a world view in which only the individual counts has led to a situation in which the planet may very soon become uninhabitable for humans.

Chi is primary, and it also encompasses technological forms.

Forces created by technological means are able to impede organic energy forms — to kill things. But they can't give birth. So I call technological forms relative forms of the chi. While they are interdependent with, and in a sense inseparable from the absolute, organic, generative chi, the relative is secondary. It can only replicate itself, or do as it's told.

The force of organic life is ultimately much stronger than the technological — because it's generative. The planet we live on, the universe which it's a tiny part of, and all the life-forms which live upon it, are composed of a generative force, and conduct it.

The balance is tipping, as ecosystems, animals and humans are dying from human stewardship of the chi as if it were something to be controlled and owned. Since the development of agriculture the concept that land, food sources and people are static, separate entities to be accumulated, traded, profited from, or forced into linear trajectories of development, has caused land, food, animals and people to be abused. This is how colonialism developed, and slavery.

The flow of chi is innately creative, free, and sexual. Sexual ownership, exploitation and abuse play a key role in the ill-health of bodies and systems. The flow, particularly of female sexual energy, needs to move freely. The same goes for the creative expression of the chi.

The flow of chi is innately about the dynamics of interdependency and a kind of fluid exchange. The act of exchange has become colonised into static units of accumulation, by the monetary system, and hyped up into a turbo-charged institutionalised machine of abuse by capitalism.

The spirit of exchange, apart from money, needs to be reanimated — a counter-move is necessary, the cultivation of more of the chi that comes alive in the interactions of soil and water, and in human hands.

So the ancient becomes revolutionary — but it isn't really old. And it's not really 'ancient things' but timelessness itself which is revolutionary — and revolutionary, at the root, means that everything goes around. All ancient indigenous understandings of time and space and humans' place within them are cyclical and multi-dimensional — they never were linear and it's only from the perspectives of linearity, progress and profit that understandings or techniques seem 'old'.

Timeless energy, unbound by any particular moment or place, working within the past and future, ancestors and future children, you and me, wherever we are, is both radical in our

13

contemporary reality — within the systems we presently live in — and radically necessary.

Awareness and cultivation of pure, timeless, natural energy is needed right now, if we're to stop this ship from sinking, and it needs to be used with clear intention.

The chi is needed to heal — which means to induce a state not of balance but of unimpeded flow. In Taoist terms, chi (life energy) plus yi (intention) equals shi — oneness with the momentum of the universe, seamless manifestation.

Healing isn't a cul de sac, an end in itself, although certain cultures have developed around it, rendering it a loop of endless practices, aimed at maintaining a consistent state of wellbeing, or even perfection, digging through layer after layer after layer to get to it. The loop is both effortful and futile, because there's no such thing as a consistent state in nature, or a single destination to get to.

So if healing is inducing a state of unimpeded flow, a dynamic fluidity, and that state of flow is the state of the primordial chi itself, we might also call healing restoration of the natural state. The natural state is both behind and within nature (the dance of yin and yang, the forms). It's inherently dynamic and creative, it pushes on, up, down and around. It destroys things and makes new things. It consists of pleasure, and pain. What's consistent is that it feels good to be alive, the flow itself feels good, has a bliss-edge, even in grief.

It's important to remember this. While healing is about restoring balance and wholeness to fragmented or imbalanced systems, that balance is not a static state of affairs but a fertile, ever-shifting one. It isn't an attainment or a resting place, at least not for long.

This fertile, dynamic state is your experience of absolute reality, you could call it the Tao, in which time and space are not linear, people are not separate and everything is in fact happening at once.

In the Taoist understanding, though, everything has two aspects, the dark and light, yin and yang. So the state of fluid interconnection has two sides. While constant interconnection with others feels generative and energising in the realm of intuitive feeling, dreams, or practices such as calling upon the presence of the ancestors, it's also true that being in constant virtual communication with many people at once tends to drain the system. Scattering and dispersing energy rather than focusing it, this form of connection causes depletion rather than recharge. Hence it's disconnecting from screens that gives you a feeling of replenishment, not connecting to more of them.

In disconnecting from screens you can ground yourself in your biological being, and charge up from a source that works — the absolute, generative source that makes that small, crucial difference between life and death. It's in the nature of energy to move and expand, so once it has space to move within your brain and heart, you can start to use it to solve some of the problems people are facing/creating, right now, for example, war, starvation, pandemics, climate emergency.

The climate emergency is an energy emergency and we actually have energy at our fingertips. Literally in our fingertips.

Once you're flowing and not impeded by your own suffering (which is everyone's suffering), freed from the endless healing loop, off you can go with the intention of changing things, unblocking the natural flow wherever you go, be it empathy or clean water.

Here is the reiki way of doing it.

INTRODUCTION

Holding my hand against your skin in just that place, the energy became so dense it was as if my hand merged into your body, and hand and body merged into the earth, and the earth merged into the core of the earth, and a force stronger than gravity held us there meshed together in space. There was no option of moving, and no time either. I have no idea how long we spent sinking into the core of the earth in that one spot, but it was probably an hour or two. Distinct surges of heat and energy moved through our bodies but within the vast pressure they were barely discernible. Suddenly, a solidity within the liver that I had not really felt as an entity before – disappeared.

This is a book about the essence of transmitting the chi according to the Reiki system, for practitioners at all levels, those who have only been on the receiving end of Reiki, those who are simply interested, and those who heal using the chi without identifying with the Reiki system. It isn't a manual and you won't find exercises or meditations described here. The practice of Reiki, as it was passed down from its originator and as it moved sideways to the West, has developed in many different ways, with additions and mergings from many other traditions. A historical and cross cultural study of Reiki is a fascinating prospect but this is not what I'm doing.

Essentially I'm sharing my own experience with the chi and how it resonates with renditions of the Reiki story itself. As this is the way (or Tao) that has appeared in front of me to walk, it's clearly as close to the source of power as I can get.

My intention is that by going deeply into my own experience rather than looking around in an investigative, comparative manner, the actual life force can be amplified and enlivened, rather than thoughts about it. By 'my own experience' I mean more than life events, I mean thoughts, feelings and experiences which come from within, and simultaneously from far beyond. They're my specific connections, my thread, the flavour of me-in-this-lifetime.

I'll be using the words 'reiki' and 'chi' sometimes interchangeably to refer to life-energy, and Reiki to refer to the specific system which has been passed down from Mikao Usui.

While I initially intended this book to be exclusively about the Reiki system, during its writing my dear friend, colleague, teacher (and co-founder of Wayward Publications) Stephen Russell, otherwise known as the Barefoot Doctor, somewhat absurdly died. By which I don't mean he died in any particularly strange way (to the contrary, he died in his sleep). But the very fact that a man who so intensely embodied aliveness in every way, and who made it his life's work to do so, and to spread the delight-in-aliveness virus, should die at the age of 65 – rather than, let's say, 165 which would have been a more appropriate absurdity.

This had a profound effect, not only on my writing style (in the last paragraph anyway!) but on the essence of the book.

Stephen did not have a lot of time for the contemporary western Reiki movement as a whole, and expressed the hope that I would 'discreetly infer' in this book that the notion of becoming enlightened in a weekend was ridiculous. He himself had learnt healing by a process of absorption from masters, who had honed their respective skills over decades, rather than acquiring certifications chosen and purchased from the marketplace.

He went on, however, to sell online courses, in order to spread the knowledge, and therefore the healing, more swiftly and widely than could be done on an in person basis. The truth is never any less than contradictory. It simply has to contain both sides, in order to be true.

The fact is that chi is energy and belongs to no particular tradition. In Taoist practice chi is intensified and channelled through cultivation practices, and then it naturally heals, as a side-effect, wherever it goes. Which is not to say that there are not methods involved – healing is one of the five excellences which make up a good life, along with meditation, martial arts, composition, and performance.

Reiki courses typically contain less rigorous and complex energy cultivation exercises, and there may be undue emphasis placed on the idea of transmission from 'one who has it' to 'one who doesn't', rather than the teaching of practices which anyone can do and the eliciting of energies which are in everyone — although some will be better at channeling it than others. This latter fact may be somewhat whitewashed in Reiki circles which focus heavily on the fact that the energy itself does what is necessary, and can do no wrong. The chi does do that, but people are more or less skilled at getting out of the way and facilitating a pure, unimpeded flow.

In the Taoist world you can do anything with the chi — fight someone for example, or throw somebody across the room without touching them. The chi in itself is raw power, and so morally neutral, yet in a gorgeous paradox, also intrinsically healing. As Stephen on his first encounter with Taoist healing wrote, 'I understood that healing was meditating and then directing the chi outwards rather than inwards' (Russell, S. 2017).

The chi is the life force, the form of Tao with which we are acquainted here on earth. The Tao, while often translated as meaning 'the Way', is quintessentially untranslatable. That's the whole point. 'The Tao which may be spoken is not the Tao' (Tao te ching). The word points towards a primordial generative force, present in everything, for which there can't be a concept, as making one would already introduce a separation. The Way is the power of nature and the natural way of things, and actions, the mind is a small conceptual device laid over it.

The chi of Taoist practice comes in two flavours, the yin and yang, associated with passive and active, masculine and feminine, dark and light, and all the binary oppositions you can think of.

The ki of reiki also comes in flavours, chanted in syllables or elicited by symbols, and, as I will explain in more detail later, there are four of them. Earth, heaven, the state of wholeness, and the state of transcendence, strongly related to Mahayana Buddhism (which incorporates the previous three and goes beyond). This for me gives the Reiki system a specific delicacy and edge.

Yet all the practices and traditions disappear so easily — the moment you fall asleep. The sheer immensity of the empty space pointed to by Buddhism, the dark matter apprehended by physics, the primordial Tao which makes the dancing sparks that you and I briefly are, put the human desire to stick to one particular story or be faithful to a particular tradition firmly into perspective.

You stick to particular practices more or less faithfully, depending on all the myriad factors that go into your individual nature. At the end of the day, in the words of the Buddhist Heart Sutra, 'form is emptiness and emptiness is form,' and some will spend their lives erring on the side of form, and others on emptiness. The emptiness referred to is not a lack but the presence of all at once, without the separation into forms — emptiness being a kind of conceptless concept akin to the Tao.

19

The Reiki symbol Ho a ze ho ne, the connection symbol, speaks to this emptiness, or more precisely it is the aspect of the energy which emphasises the fact that emptiness and form do not differ from each other. It is the not-differing itself which flies into focus here, which lights me up, which makes me into a stronger conductor for the energy. And this is the point I would like to transmit along my way.

A note about secrecy

According to Reiki tradition, the symbols for the different kinds of energy are kept in strict secrecy and passed down to students only at the appropriate stage. I have not revealed the symbols here, but I have made the sacred sounds from which the symbols derive available. My sense, from meditation and in my own thinking, is that this is appropriate for the rapidly moving and very difficult times we are living in. I also feel sure (I hope I am not mistaken!) that people cannot be harmed or harm others by using these particular sound waves without really being attuned to them, or following the precepts. The sound seems to cut through all error. Also, some people may immediately and intuitively use advanced kotodama to great benefit, and I feel they should have the chance to do so.

CHAPTER ONE –

THE REIKI SYSTEM –

OVERVIEW AND FOUNDATION

Reiki is a system, or may be better described as an organic entity, which was conceived by, or crystallised in the life of, Mikao Usui, its founder. Usui was a practitioner of Tendai Buddhism, Shintoism (involving energy practices which have a significant crossover with Taoism), and Shugendo (mountain asceticism). He called what he practiced and taught, 'Method to Achieve Personal Perfection', or simply 'My system' (King, 2005), or the 'Usui system for connecting with your ancestral self through the body-mind' (Rivard, 2007).

The name Reiki appeared once the method was eventually transmitted to the West. I am not going to recount here the history of how the Reiki lineage extended to the West, gathering the flavours first of Christianity, and then of the New Age. My aim is to stay with the roots of the system and water them a little more, as it seems to me that we need the raw power of this system now, and that the roots, and how they have travelled through history, sometimes in the open, sometimes in disguise, always implicitly alive, are where that power is.

Hand healing, or 'teate' had been traditionally present in Japanese culture since ancient times, and in Usui's understanding, it was the cultivation of spiritual insight, through energy practices and ethics, that instigated it. Healing was understood to take place essentially through intuition and intention. Usui is said to have empowered his students simply by looking at them. In Taoist terms, chi (life energy) plus yi (intention) equals shi — oneness with the momentum of the universe, seamless manifestation. Intention equals result.

What Usui called 'My System' was a combination of hand healing, precepts with a strong Buddhist flavour, some specially chosen Waka poems (by Emporer Meiji), empowerments known as reiju, also reminiscent of Buddhist empowerments and blessings, mantras known as kotodama in traditional Japanese practices, or represented by symbols (to be chanted or visualised, respectively), and meditations and chi-cultivating techniques.

The combination of these elements, and their common presence each in the others, produced a uniquely powerful blend, simple in delivery and deep in resonance, and composed of the deepest insight and experience (insight and experience being essentially the same, rather than divided as they are in the Western philosophical tradition).

Divorced from such deep and consistent spiritual practice, Reiki in the Western world can present as a shallow mishmash of new age components chosen at random, a well-intentioned feel-good placebo, based on a kind of blind faith, with not much skill involved. Placebo of course is the most powerful healing effect there is, and that comes down to the power of the subconscious mind, aka the Tao. But that's for another time.

In fact, at the root, what we call Reiki is a spontaneous culmination of spiritual practices, and more particularly of the dedication, focus and concentration of one individual, who scooped them into one system. Within this particular vibration of the life energy that everything is composed of, there are four specifically distinguished, distinct flavours.

The first is the flavour of earth, a raw, material power; the second is sky/heaven, the breath of spirit; the third is the subtle energy of connection between the earth and sky, or to be more precise, the sense in which they are nondivisible; the fourth flavour is the key, a total condensation of all the kinds of energy — total illumination, as understood by Mahayana Buddhists and encapsulated in one of their foundational texts, the Heart Sutra — 'form does not differ from emptiness, emptiness does not differ from form'. This realisation of the actual state of reality is associated with groundlessness and bright light.

It is this insight/experience of nonduality that enables Reiki to be practiced long distance (using the 'connection' aspect of the reiki). Linear, measurable distance and time are, on the absolute level, illusory. You aren't 'sending' Reiki from one place to another, you're entering the connection(less) state, the dimension in which all places and times co-exist.

The final/central/most direct realisation of life force, in the fourth aspect, facilitates the transmission of the skill of chanelling Reiki from master to student.

Let's go to the precepts now, in translation from the manual Usui used for his students:

The Secret Method for Inviting Blessings/to Invite Happiness

The Spiritual Medicine of Many Illnesses/The Miracle Medicine for All Diseases

For today only, anger not,

worry not. With appreciation

Do your work. Be kind to people.

In your life, do gassho as your mind recalls.

Precepts may appear, especially to those from monotheistic religions, like rules for conduct, yet they differ fundamentally. It might seem as if 'the secret of inviting happiness through many blessings' (King, 2005) is merely a poetic way of phrasing 'do this in order to be happy and well', but the picture is far more nuanced than this.

Maybe conducting yourself in a way which is morally good is the secret to happiness. Maybe what is good makes you happy by definition. This would link goodness and happiness in a radically different way from that in which the Judeo-Christian tradition does.

Following these ethical principles isn't like following a rule, but like finding, or unlocking a secret, opening a doorway. Happiness isn't a product of these behaviours, in any kind of technical sense, but rather it's invited in this way. We can't get it, acquire it or produce it, and we don't control it, we can only issue an invitation, and then it comes by itself, if it so chooses, when the way is clear.

The next step is that this happiness is invited to come, not through cause and effect but through blessings. There is a something sacred, completely beyond us, which bestows them. This something does not need to be defined, and couldn't be, but the sense of blessing is fundamental to the system, and it can be felt. It is quite intimately linked to the precept 'be humble' (King, 2005) or 'with appreciation'. In contemporary self-help humbleness and appreciation appear in the form of an emphasis on gratitude.

The next point implied is that the ways of being which constitute secrets to inviting happiness also constitute medicine. A direct line is drawn between ethical ways of being, happiness, blessings, and health. The moral, psychological, spiritual and physical worlds are all intertwined, inter-existing. In a sense, all one reality.

Mikao Usui followed these precepts, with their strong flavour of Tendai Buddhism, and practiced Buddhism and Shintoism side by side. He studied martial arts, so was intimately acquainted with cultivation of the chi in the Taoist sense, as well as kiko, a Japanese energy cultivation practice, and swordsmanship. He undertook three years of Zen practice, starting in 1922.

Using meditation, mantras and chanting kotodama, a Japanese term meaning word spirits, he reached a point when, after 21 days fasting and meditation, on Mount Kurama in 1923, he experienced the state of total illumination pointed towards in the Heart Sutra (the fundamental text of Mahayana Buddhism) – gate gate paragate parasamgate bodhi svaha — 'gone, gone, gone beyond, gone completely beyond, awake at last!' This state is beyond the illusion of separate, unchanging things, which causes suffering.

The flood of physical/spiritual energy Usui experienced in this state, the culmination of intense focus on spiritual practice, was healing by its very nature. This was not the purpose of it, it was a naturally co-existing property. Joy, light, healing all came at once, as subtly different aspects of the chi.

Another inherent quality of the energy was that it demanded to be shared. Usui started study groups, in which he initiated others into Reiki. He did this through 'reiju', which means spiritual gift, a practice with its origins in Buddhist empowerments, or transmissions from teacher to student. Usui performed this reiju by simply looking at the student and intending that they receive.

The students were also guided in meditation and chanting, with 6-9 month periods of time dedicated to chanting each kotodama in order to immerse their whole being in the energy of each spirit — the earth, sky, connection, and finally the key to total illumination. This total immersion is important. It ensures that the practice isn't just used as an additional tool but entails the student experiencing the disappearance of the self they had identified with, and what happens next.

Kotodama

The word spirits, kotodama, chanted are an ancient and foundational part of Japanese culture, a type of mantra practice in the Shinto religion, based on the belief that words manifest power. As the world is constituted by sound vibrations, not all of which are audible to humans, it makes sense that particular vibrations should resonate with particular states of mind and body — they actually constitute different states.

Mikao Usui was seeped in the kotodama. And the original Reiki system also included Waka, traditional Japanese poems. In these poems, meditative states are implied by concentration on the present moment and the physical world, and the words themselves conjure the magnetic force fields of those elements.

Visible symbols to represent these force fields were introduced only later. Usui began teaching his system in 1915. In 1923 a huge earthquake erupted in Japan, and Usui went into action, healing the injured. He also taught healing techniques to the Imperial officers from the army, so that they could heal greater numbers of people, more swiftly, and pass their skills on to others. Skills had to be transmitted fast and effectively, there was no time for a long, gradual spiritual development process and the officers were not necessarily interested in undertaking it. To solve this problem, Usui used symbols as visual aids or short cuts to the energy experience that previous students had cultivated over time.

It seems to me vital to preserve the non-sectarian and practical spirit of the original Reiki teachings. As Reiki is passed on by personal teaching and transmission, rather than academic learning — like the schools of Buddhism from which it was birthed — preservation of the original spirit is integral to the whole endeavour. It's the whole point.

This, while it may seem paradoxical, also means that faithfulness to the true original spirit involves an organic growth of Reiki in every single individual practitioner, and a difference in its nature. As people are different, once the spirit moves through them, the Reiki practice will necessarily be different too, in a palpable sense, just as perfume smells different on different people.

The spirit of the precepts is gentle, but they're also tough. They constitute the causes and conditions for happiness and health. Not ways in which happiness or health can be acquired or produced, but basic conditions that need to be in place, and ways of 'inviting'. The invitation needs to be sincere, and then the natural state is not blocked, but free to flourish, and happiness may arrive by itself.

Then again, it might not. If you're in the throes of pain or grief — you won't be feeling happy. That would be unnatural. Yet many blessings may still be invited, may still come.

The spiritual medicine might not cure the physical illness.

We're all going to die.

But it cures the spiritual 'illnesses' that occur when you get lost in anger, worry, pride, dishonesty, and cruelty to self/others.

What is an illness anyway? You could call it a cluster or system of habitual, entrenched processes that cause distress to the organism. A particular constellation of processes or blocks is given a name, as if it were a single, invasive thing, which arrived from outside and attacked the individual (another single thing).

In fact, if habitual processes are noticed as such, rather than made into invasive entities in the mind, they tend to loosen their grip and pass in their own time, without additional suffering. This is the case for processes which are primarily physical, mental or emotional — in fact these are inseparable.

The first two precepts work on the principle of loosening the grip, applying it to anger and worry — which seem to be naturally occurring phenomena — as habitual processes. Let's take them one by one.

Precepts in detail

1. Just for today, do not anger

You may have a natural impulse to protect self or others, which comes along with a flash of adrenaline and the energy required to do so. However, by adding a mental narrative to this impulse, you can quickly turn the story into a distress-maintaining and harm-provoking habit, which effectively prevents you from acting on the causes of the situations which made you angry in the first place. Angry mental narratives often move in the direction of reinforcing to yourself how right you are and how wrong others are.

Anger as a habitual process moves on a continuum from hypervigilance and readiness to protect yourself, to throwing responsibility for anything unwanted onto others and trying to destroy it/them. Anger is a strong energy that can cause harm to others when expressed outwardly, or to yourself if it's suppressed.

There's clearly a lot of injustice causing suffering in the world and many situations in which an anger response appropriately arises.

The anger energy may bring strength and power to act in the situation, or it may stress and deplete you, depending on the kind of noise you make in your head in relation to the situation, the quality of the energy you feed. A chronic mental-anger pattern will keep you stuck in your own head. Both in your thinking and in the external world, you become trapped in repetitive dynamics in which nothing changes.

2. Just for today, do not worry

Worrying may be the most common mental commentary you're in the habit of engaging in. It has a masterful way of keeping you from being present, and runs on a delusion that by thinking about things which are going to happen, might have happened, or have already happened, you exert control over those things, and keep yourself and others safe from harm.

Worrying spins explanations for states of anxiety in the body, ranging from the plausible to the wild. It stops you realising the cause of your fear directly, bringing all kinds of plausible explanations into the mix. The problem is that on the mental level alone, there's no way of working out which explanation is true, for sure. There will always be arguments, and counter-arguments, and doubts, you'll never know for sure what if...? The mind, left to its own devices, without being treated as one with the body, the emotions, the spirit, without the flow of the chi, also works on the delusion that it can find rational proof, to the point of 100% certainty, for its thesis, if it just works hard enough. This is both futile and exhausting.

You might also have learned, from experiences in childhood, usually by picking up on how your parents behaved, to conflate worrying with care. If worrying is an expression of love then it's easy to conclude that not worrying about someone means you don't care about them.

In contemporary Western society, the over-valuing of rationality and proof, and the default treatment of people as separate, isolated units has given plenty of fuel to the habit of worrying.

Stating the intention not to worry, and allowing this intention to permeate your life, just for one day, not only brings relief and releases energy, but also works to dismantle the power structures based on those misguided concepts — that you are a separate, isolated unit, reliant on judgements and ideas that are produced in isolation from feelings, bodily sensations, intuitions, and the flow of chi.

Dismantling these concepts leads to liberation.

3. be humble/with appreciation

The command to be humble is also a suggestion that one mental narrative in particular should be given up - the one which centres directly on yourself. A lot of energy typically goes into keeping up the edifice of your identity, wrestling yourself into the shape of the kind of person you think you are, or should be, stoking up your pride or conversely getting lost in shame or judgements of yourself. All of this reinforces your own self-importance. When you let go of it, and stop making such a big deal out of yourself, whether as a good thing or a bad thing, the chi can flow naturally. This has beneficial effects on you and everyone around you. The main point is simply that the chi can flow unimpeded, as strongly as possible, when the ego is not in the way.

4. be honest in your work/do your work

At this point, after three precepts directed at your 'inner' world, the fourth precept steps in to bring you firmly into the 'external', the material world you live in. It's not only about what happens in your head. Work is the energy exchange that ensures your material survival, and the way in which you provide services or give energy to others. It's the way interdependence works.

If this exchange happens in an exploitative way, at the root is, once again, the conceptual picture of people, organisations, or structures being made up of separate units, with opposing and competing interests. Once again, acting according to this belief impedes the natural circulation of the chi.

For this reason, being honest with what you make, do, contribute and exchange in the outer, physical world is of fundamental importance. Any kind of manipulation distorts the flow.

5. be compassionate to yourself and others/be kind to people

Without this one, there's just no way the chi can be experienced as a clear flow between people. It doesn't work without the fluid engagement of the warm, loving energy of the heart. Or to be more precise, for humans, chi *is* the fluid, warm, loving energy of the heart. There seems to be no logical reason why this should be so, yet it is. Without love there's no life. No human baby, born helpless, would survive without care.

Without intentional care there's no survival, and no healing. And when you experience compassionate love, no difference is perceived between self and others. So there's no reason to single yourself out among the human race for worse treatment, and similarly no need to judge other people harshly.

The precepts aren't prerequisites, or boxes to be ticked before practicing Reiki, they're integral elements of the system — results of practice, and inherent in the energy itself. They're neither external, nor internal to your 'personal life'. If you're not following the precepts, while you may be using the life force in some technical way, you're not practicing Reiki.

The precepts provide clear instructions for setting 'yourself' aside in order for the chi to flow freely. You remain very much the particular human being that you are, in the form of your specific nature, shaped by your experiences, your biology, but the 'self' identity composed of the set of anger and worry-narratives that keep you defined, and ultimately isolated by, your own stories — generally about the past and the future — is set aside. A whole collection of behaviours — how you behave when you believe you're an isolated being, superior to others, or when you're not working according to your values, when you're unkind to yourself and other people — all this is set aside. That might seem a huge undertaking but we're reminded, it's just a commitment for today.

Setting aside the illusion that people are solid, permanent, isolated individual entities, which need to attach to or reject other entities in order to maintain their existence, is the only way, according to Buddhism, in which suffering can be cut off at the root.

When following the Reiki precepts, you live with less suffering — without the exhausting and depressing effort of self-maintenance. You can actually relax, and use the energy that used to be scrunched up within mental stories (whether or not they were based on fact) and your emotional reactions to them. As the stress is released, that energy becomes available for use in the present moment. At the end of the day, the present moment is all we have.

do gassho every morning and evening/in your life, do gassho as your mind recalls

The fact that the principles are to be practiced, not just held theoretically, is stressed by the final, according to the most common translation, 'Do gassho every morning and evening/Keep in your mind and recite'. According to the Rivard translation, 'In your life, do gassho as your mind recalls'. This may seem less demanding and more flexible, but it points I think towards performing gassho more often, possibly many times a day, every time you think of it, rather than it being a ritual which you might carry out as a habit, without necessarily engaging with it.

Gassho refers to a simple kneeling position with hands held together as if in prayer, and awareness placed on the energy flowing through them. This is a simple and basic meditation practice, a kind of mental hygiene which is necessary at the start and end of the day, a practical way to take care of and clean the mind, in the same way as you do your body on rising and going to bed. If you can find the time to clean your teeth, and remember it every day, then you can clean your mind.

keep in mind and recite

Keeping in mind and reciting refers to the practice of mantras and chanting (silently or aloud), or maybe in more contemporary terms, to an active and intentional reprogramming of the subconscious mind.

In order to reprogramme the narratives that run your own version of reality, at a level more fundamental than argument, the level at which it appears to you that things just are, repetition is required as well as receptivity — much repetition. It's not enough just to have a flash of insight and realise or understand something — let alone everything! — once.

This insight simply won't remain in a mind which is constantly churning the old narratives and beliefs over and over — reminding you what kind of a person you are, what you can and can't do, what the world is like. Whether you give a generous interpretation to the perpetual production of limiting, or downright negative beliefs, seeing them trying to keep you safe in an uncertain world, or whether you regard them as sadistic attempts to bring you down at every turn, it's incontrovertible that they're always squandering large amounts of energy that could be better used on direct action.

In order to change these stories and the beliefs inherent in them, to teach yourself that anger and fear are not necessary or helpful, you need to repeat the new intentions until they become the default, the background, the obvious. Keep in mind and recite.

CHAPTER TWO

LIFE IN PRACTICE/ PRACTICE IN LIFE

I became a Reiki master after twenty years of training — but the vast majority of this training took place without my consciously engaging in anything called Reiki. In fact to be honest I pretty much forgot that I'd done the first and second degrees back in my early twenties, beautiful though the experiences of these attunements, in the very special town of Glastonbury, were at the time.

I continued, though, to nourish my spiritual medicine, meandering through many different forms. I read texts and meditated with groups from various Buddhist traditions, as I came across them. I never felt entirely aligned with any group, but there were always individual encounters within them which fed the spark. Each time something was carried forward, a new strand of energy, of aliveness, sureness. Those sparks and strands made up a practice, gathering its own momentum, which fed something in me I hadn't known was hungry.

I was living in Poland during those years, in an isolated and traditional rural area. I learned the language as fast as I could in order to do work that was meaningful for me — as a therapist, rather than teaching English. I integrated with varying degrees of success into a new family, town, culture, country. My then husband and I were bringing up two daughters.

I wanted to do this as a mammal does, which involved breastfeeding and sleeping with my daughters until they wanted to stop doing so – which was longer than I initially anticipated! This was an extension of protective, nourishing chi to my children, a kind of energetical contact which is the only way to make true contact with a newborn, but for older children is an unusual frequency. This might have been represented by a sound frequency or a mantra. It was a kind of practice.

I kept writing, including a PhD thesis on the concept of the self/no-self in therapy, from the points of view of Buddhist philosophy and Gendlin's philosophy of the implicit. Writing was always about the flow of the chi, getting myself into a state in which it could flow through me easily in the forms of words. The required structure of a PhD thesis was challenging to my normal process - first flow and then editing. The new practice involved structuring the flow from the start, making different channels in advance. Some engineering was involved.

Then, one day, the surplus arrived. A vast amount of energy circulating around my body, shooting through the crown so it felt as if someone were putting a cigarette out on the top of my head, burning my feet and flowing through my hands to such an extent that I was compelled to place them on people, to relieve the pressure, and to spread the healing.

I didn't really recognise this as a 'thing', or name it. It quickly became just a part of my everyday life. I would place my hands on the people who were nearest. I developed a connection during this time, involving many passages of growth, from the painful to the ecstatic and most of the shades inbetween, which resulted in our joining forces to set up a healing refuge on a large piece of wild, secluded land.

terrealuma, the name for the place which finally came to us (after a long and fruitless struggle to 'think it up') was built out of intentional engagement and dance with the chi.

The land itself is extraordinarily powerful, and it has its own practices — although they are not geographically native —

Buddhist chanting, and Taoist manifestation and methods of working, dancing, playing with, nurturing, and cultivating the chi. From internal alchemy to the shadow boxing form Pa Kua, otherwise known as the dance of the I Ching, the chi moves through the land, the work, the weather, the vision, the ancestors, the past, those who come and go, to help, to be nourished, and each other. It is directly expressed in healing, in chanting, and in music, with hands and voices.

This mix of elements and methods is very similar to those from which Mikao Usui shaped the original Reiki system, including the four different aspects of the chi originally elicited and embodied by chanting the kotodama. This is how all the various kinds of sound healing work, from Tibetan singing bowls, to mantra chanting. More of the power of chanting in my life will come later.

As a poet and writer I've always been aware of the magnetic force field of words, and worked in the original Reiki way, with intent and intuition, to conjure something with words which lies between a sound, a vision and a feeling — something that the philosopher and therapist Gendlin, the founder of focusing, called a felt sense. Gendlin's work has been a pivotal thread in my thinking since I first encountered it during my training as a therapist.

A felt sense is a crystallisation of the uncountable crossings, interweavings and blockings of all the life processes that have ever happened - in the concrete, specific way they inter-affect and interact in you and your situation right now.

In everyday life you're probably quick to interpret your experience through your mental apparatus, or if that seems inappropriate, to dive straight into feelings. Both these habits can be quite draining. A more energising and creative way is to go by that felt sense that you can't quite put your finger on or explain, yet which contains, usually in a physically sensed way, all the factors feeding into the situation that we could not explicate if we tried (a human life would be too short).

Engagement with, and living from, the felt sense is energising in the sense that energy is not lost trying to wrestle reality into rational sense, or emotional comfort, and living this way is creative in the sense that you can feel everything which has ever existed implicit in the moment – and what is relevant at this precise second, what wishes to go forward. This relevancy contains so many interactions and connections, any of which can be brought into relief — the possibilities for creating art are literally infinite.

For me the felt sense is a perfect way of conceptualising that inbetween place in which all that's unquantifiable may be sensed — it has always been the guiding spirit of my poetry, it constitutes the whole difference between writing a poem and writing a text which simply expresses an idea, thought or feeling.

Direct experience of the unquantifiable, the power of the inbetween places, sensed within my body was also the essence of the Taoist inner alchemy practices I learned from Stephen Russell, and I combined it into my own mix with the manifestation technique he taught, where attention and intention are brought to the aspect of this unquantifiable energy which is identical within my body and in the external world, past, present and future. When I performed this combination, barefoot in the dry yellow grass in the area of terrealuma where the earth had been scooped and landscaped into the shape of an amphitheatre, I felt so much a part of the intrinsic primordial power of the universe that frankly it was scary.

Such heat arose, spilling from the palms of my hands, the soles of my feet and the crown of my head that sometimes I couldn't stand it, it was, once more, as if someone were grinding a cigarette out on the top of my head, as if my hands and feet were on the verge of explosion — spontaneous combustion did not seem a distant concept. I would ask Stephen what to do, feeling that something had to be wrong. This wasn't very balanced! Surely this was insane!

'Great' he said, or something very similar, 'heal more people'.

Placing my hands on people with healing intention served to ground me, as if their bodies were lightning conductors. It provided them with healing, as it naturally gravitated to areas of need, and with energy – the raw material to perform their own internal arts.

Placing my hands on myself enabled my body to clarify internally, to the extent that several potentially serious health conditions cleared up completely. Test results came back clear for no reason that was apparent to the doctors. It was just as well I had refused the hysterectomy and the lifelong taking of hormones. Neither were even remotely necessary. I also lost a lot of weight, just through the energy burning and clarifying its way through me. I prefer the word clarifying to cleansing. It wasn't that I was dirty inside before. It was more messy, blocking itself. At this time I had consciously 'forgotten' about Reiki and the two attunements I had received. I rediscovered the source from another angle, brought to me by my own changing life, my changing body, my desire not to get caught up in any schemes or methods which didn't feel radically authentic to me, as much a part of me as my own skin. This had not been the case in the way I was initiated into Reiki in my twenties, so that outer casing was left behind, as I shed one skin, got messed up again, and discovered once more a way to peel myself raw and contact the source, to come alive and clear and stay in motion.

I had been meditating, for many years, without obvious effect on the energy flow in my body. My head became clearer, my heart warmer, but there was still plenty of opportunity in my system for blockages, stuckness and confusion on denser levels, especially in the lower Tantien, my lower belly, the very centre of my power.

Neglect of my own power source during the years of bringing up children, and being naturally and primarily oriented to others' needs, turned out to be nearly fatal. Running off a power that was never consciously re-sourced, clearing only my mental and emotional states without dealing directly with my body, or with the wholeness of it all, or the fundamental energy from which the mental and emotional derive... this left me not-present in the most important of ways, leading to confusion in my relationships and exhaustion on all fronts. I needed to reclaim my body, the denser, palpable levels of physical and sexual energy (this is not a big part of Reiki theory but sexual energy is exactly the same as the life energy chi, so the Taoists would say), I needed to flood my body with attention, intention, giving it my explicit permission to clarify, wake up, release the energy that was stuck there, abandoned, artificially isolated, in a solid, dense, material dream of isolation. It all needed to come home, all of me needed to come home.

This process kickstarted for me, as for many, around the age of forty. Life threw up some clarifying experiences and my energy awoke to meet them. The illnesses which had been festering had to meet the challenge, they fell away from the new light and aliveness within my body.

And with the crazy surplus, I decided to do as my teacher suggested, and use it to heal people, in the most natural way, just putting my hands on them, the easy way, the way Jesus did, the witches did, and so many others, calling others home when they asked me for help, which they did, as we can all sniff out energy, and we all, deep down, beneath our armour and our addictions, crave more of it, more aliveness.

Then it was the turn of my voice to come to life. It happened also as a part of the creation of terrealuma, the physical place in which the healing was arising. I was introduced to the practice of chanting the Japanese mantra of Nicheren Buddhism, Nam Myoho Renge Kyo. It is intended to bring about blessings in your life in a very tangible sense, the power of intention and manifestation are very present here, as is the sense of contacting the raw power of the universe. In fact, Nicheren Buddhism takes chanting practice to the ultimate level — regarding the practice as necessary and sufficient to manifest the enlightened state here and now in this lifetime.

While I was familiar with some of the traditional Buddhist mantras, particularly the Heart Sutra in sanskrit — gate gate paragate, parasamgate bodhi svaha, and the Tibetan Buddhist mantra of Alokitesvara, the boddhisattva who hears the cries of the world and the expression of her compassion, Om mani padme hung, Nam myoho renge kyo felt very different.

While the heart sutra opened up the mental and spiritual space wide, and Om mani padme hung created a spacious warmth and comfort in the heart, I felt secondary effects in my body but they were just that, effects. The main workings of the mantras were not physical, not within the life energy itself as energy (which then encompasses all things).

Nam Myoho Renge Kyo may be translated as 'I dedicate myself to the mystical law of cause and effect with the sound of my voice'.

This is what is needed. The element of dedication (intention), the understanding (of the simple logic of cause and effect and acknowledgment of the vast implications of this), and actually making a physical sound which expresses this dedication and understanding. Not reproducing a sound but making the sound of your own voice, your own particular, distinct and unique combination of factors, your own precious human life.

I dedicate myself. It has the power of intention. It awakes the power of the body and the oneness of that with the mystical law, or way, with the implicit intricacy, the Tao, or whatever name it is you use for everything.

I dedicate myself [...]

41

with the sound of my voice. My voice. My very own sound frequency vibration, with which I express and communicate. My frequency which adds to all the rest of the frequencies that make up matter. The part of my frequency which I can control, and which I can link to meaning. The sound of my intention as it meets all the other intentions and expressions and communications in the world. This is what I choose to do with it. Dedicate myself to the mystery, to the law which holds firm — cause and effect. What I do is never without effect, everything produces an effect. Hence, I vow to take care with my actions, to produce more clarity and more healing in a world of suffering and mess. With the sound of my voice.

It turned out that my voice could make sounds I had no idea existed once I started to chant. It turned out that these sounds massaged me internally and also externally beyond my own body. Sometimes they seemed to belong to other humans, who were no longer alive, sometimes they did not seem human at all. I was never remotely concerned by anything while chanting, there was no space for mental clutter or emotional pain. It was full on power. Hence - I got the overflow and the heat again, hands, feet, crown of the head. The surplus of energy poured out of me and off me like water in the shower. It was there to radiate and to be given. I carried on.

These were the roots. And then I remembered the Reiki.

The Reiki came back, cyclically, although it had never been away. My mind joined up to my body again. My body joined up to my mind again. It became an unstoppable flow to others, people and things and plans and intentions and dreams. Power and motion.

I started singing. An old friend got in touch and asked me to write some lyrics for his music. I had always wanted to sing but I was convinced that I couldn't, because the sound didn't match up with the voices of singers I admired, or because I just did not believe I had access to beauty and power through my voice. I went to singing lessons. I was taught basically Taoist energy practices, moving breath and energy, by a singing professional who had never heard of Taoism. She was an expert. Names don't matter. She was also a Reiki master although she may not have heard of that either.

Learning to sing was an experience of the particular movements of the chi and their resonance within and between the three internal energy chambers, or Tantiens, in the belly, chest and head. The microcosmic orbit, or energy channel, or loop, from the perineum up the spine to the crown then down again to meet once more between the legs, is also used in singing. The whole energy system within the body is activated, with the sound of my voice.

Being in my teacher's field, as she showed me the movements of breath and energy that I needed to use, anchoring it in the lower Tantien and circulating it around the microcosmic orbit, or, as she called it, 'putting my hood up!', I was healed and activated, activated and healed. I also discovered that singing happens through you when you make the right conditions, just like everything else does. That singing is also a practice of energy cultivation and as such as healing effects built in, inseparable.

The first way I learned to tell that a note was a good one was because of the buzzing in my teeth and crackling electricity in my fingertips. Victoria my teacher got used to these signs with admirable openmindedness. Singing for me became the cutting edge of my practice, constantly topping me up with the healing energy I used on friends and family in a hands-on capacity and at work as a therapist with clients in a more general way, maybe akin to how Usui worked, through cultivating my own field and intention for each person to receive what they need. When working with clients I was often alerted to issues by energy rushes within my own body — their supressed anger for example usually makes its first appearance in the room in my feet. Not that I share this with clients, but I have learned to work with the energy in my body during what looks like normal talking therapy, with some beautiful results. Person centred therapy, which I practice, involves the therapist providing three conditions: unconditional positive regard for the client, empathy and congruence, being authentically herself. The theory is that when these conditions are held, with the intention of healing, then the client's life force or 'actualising tendency' will be able to work its own healing. This is obviously extremely compatible with the way in which Reiki conceptualises the world, and the way it works.

I then moved on to making music involving chanting, at terrealuma. This brought the power of mantra and music together in an extremely exciting and condensed form. The energy within me grew and grew, and was now reaping rewards back in its own currency, in my own life. It's hard to say exactly how the pieces were composed − I had the sense that my parts in them arrived, they were delivered to me and all traces of the moment in which they arrived were immediately erased, almost as if to remove the possible distraction. Then I gave these co-ordinates to my musical partner who was actually a musician and could bring them to life. I would say for instance 'this starts from the bass and there's a didgeridoo' and then later in the process I would have a fuzzy felt sense of what other elements were needed — something brighter for example, in a kind of brightness that includes all kinds of sharpness and colour and articulation, something flatter... and when he produced those elements (often I hadn't even mentioned them) I had the sense of recognition — that's it, that's what it was, what I already heard, it all matches up, or it all comes home. Linear time, and the differences between our different minds, in the context of this creation, sink into the background, an irrelevance.

Making the music was an experience of connection. Connection presupposes separation. It doesn't feel, when you're within the experience, that there is any separation, but it's also true that as in the Taoist framework the yin and yang are always at play, always dancing, the forms are as real as the emptiness. With each piece of music that I was involved in, it came to me as a felt sense, as energy without form, emptiness, waiting for the musician to give it form.

Meanwhile Stephen started to spend all his time and energy on devising healing frequencies with which he produced music including affirmations, both top line and subliminal. Listening to these I was once again flooded by exactly what I needed on the level which I needed it. The bringing together of declarations and the subconscious mind with healing frequencies apart from and beyond language was once again extremely resonant with my Reiki roots.

The final piece was when I decided to become a Reiki master, through the fact that my clinical supervisor just happened to be one, and was eager to attune me, as she was aware that in my somewhat haphazard and intuitive way I had done the Reiki training necessary. I was so intimate with the energy that it was hard for me to call it something, something other than me or something other than the namelessness that was me when I was accessing full awareness of it, and being so much bigger, more complex, subtle and vast, all-encompassing really, than the 'me' I typically am.

Stephen would call this the Tao of Sarah, what I am when dwelling in the back of me, the back brain, the unconscious, an unconscious which is more than personal, a collective, ancestral unconscious, that stretches further, beyond even the human, the primordial energy I am made of, and can feel, physiologically, by dropping my energy and attention into the back area of my body. An instant state of power, energy and meditation arises.

I expected the Reiki master training to feel a little odd to me, but it turned out that my Reiki master/mistress, Heather, had just ordered a Reiki master teaching manual by Taggart King.

And this is where I learned that Mikao Usui's path and Reiki practice had also been intuitive, made up of different traditions, including sound vibrations as a foundational practice and actually nothing to do with matching up to symbols or keeping to specific set, taught, linear procedures.

I had come home, yet again.

The kotodama were the missing link for me within Reiki — it had been strong enough in itself to heal, to put me into resonance and alignment, to move my energy, but somehow had lacked a flavour of groundedness for me, and a creative spark. Once voice activation was added to Reiki I felt a whole new depth come into play – it felt ever-moving yet complete.

It felt ever-moving and complete.

So, I started to practice Reiki for the first time — after over two decades of growing intimacy and experience of the energy — taking money for sessions and treating strangers as well as friends. Taking money for the energy itself is not right, as it isn't mine — yet taking money in exchange for my time and effort is an appropriate way of ensuring my livelihood.

In the practice of Pa Kua, a fighting form which is also the dance of the I Ching, you walk the circles of the decades of your life, first one way, counter clockwise, releasing what needs to be released from that time, then the other, clockwise, charging it with energy. Each change in direction is marked by a fighting move.

It seems at this point that I'm circling with many circles already implicit in the move. Physical healing, words, music, form and emptiness, connection and aloneness/being everything.

When energy comes through me it has a taste, a flavour, a sound, a colour. It also has a degree of density. Often when people send me energy, whether they mean to or not, these days, their energy feels too dense and heavy than is

46

comfortable. There's no point attaching a mental or verbal interpretation to this. It belongs to an entirely different realm, a primary one. It's the stuff from which interpretations are made, but on the level of giving and receiving energy, it's best to keep energy being its own language.

And energy is indeed, its own language. I understand the main building blocks of the Reiki system as four energy-words. The same language speaks in three different 'things', aspects, shades of the whole.

Or, the same speech apparatus speaks three different languages, each word containing a whole language of its own. As energy may appear and be measured as either a wave or a particle depending on the design of the experiment, the chi which is one and indivisible may be elicited and experienced in different ways according to the experimental stance of the practitioner, and in the case of original Reiki, the mantra which elicits a particular form of the energy, which is probably a question of resonance, everything that exists being a different form of sound wave.

Form is emptiness and emptiness is form, and this encompasses everything. Understanding this is the story of my life.

CHAPTER THREE

REIKI IS NOT A THING

In 'Focusing is Not a Thing' (2020) I wrote:

'There seems to me to be an inherent danger in organisational and professional situations. Operational terms begin to be used to quantify and organise skills, which are inherently unquantifiable, and people — who are also inherently unquantifiable! When such a situation is applied to focusing, whose entire purpose is to dwell in and articulate the unquantifiable, a potentially alarming paradox arises'.

The same applies, quintessentially, to Reiki. The entire purpose of Reiki is to dwell in, and directly work with, the unquantifiable energy which everything ultimately is. So the aforementioned paradox remains not only somewhat absurd, as people lay their conditions upon something which is so very much 'bigger' than them in every way, but alarming too, as people with their limited understanding and need to maintain their egos intrude upon the very essence of healing and usually quite inadvertently add to the unnecessary suffering in the world. How does this work?

'According to Buddhist tenets, the maintenance of individual identities as solid, fixed things is the basic mistake, and the maintenance of group identities is an extension of that mistake. This mistake is the foundational cause of suffering, leading people to be permanently dissatisfied as they try to make life stable and unchanging. The diversion of attention towards maintenance of identity is also at the expense of the tasks we have at hand.

When treating a certain bundle of processes as a thing works against the absolute truth, rather than along with it, this causes extra confusion/suffering. All suffering is caused by a mismatch of levels. Hence, treating people as fixed, boundaried units with identities is an important way of respecting their integrity as human beings. That level must be present. But it can become intrusive when it encroaches into intimate, spiritual or creative areas, into how we truly experience our lives'. (Luczaj, 2020)

Reiki is a word which has come to represent a fluid and organic system of spiritual, healing practice that grew within and expressed itself through, or was simply inseparable from the life of Mikao Usui. Of course as we are all in essence inseparable, we can all resonate with this system as it comes to us and as it touches us, and carry that resonance and therefore the system forward in our own ways. This would be a form of organic growth.

It seems that Usui taught others intuitively and spontaneously, within the extremely firm container of the precepts, the mantras and the basic energy practices involving meditation, the breath and the hara. Rather than offering a set course of education or training, he started with himself, cultivated energy and wisdom to the point at which he simply became healing to others, then once people came to him for healing he empowered them, through the simple reiju empowerments, to do their own healing between visits to him. The reiju empowerments were an extension of the energy exercises (more a form of calling awareness to the energy and bathing in it than producing or directing it) with the power of intention, that the receiver join the flow and be able to do so by themselves. Often Usui bestowed empowerments in the style of Tendai Buddhist teachers bestowing blessings – by intention alone.

He then passed on the precepts, energy exercises and mantras, but not in a systematic, linear or necessarily linear way. He would teach the students what was required for each individual at each particular time. He might teach hand positions for self-healing, or he might not. We can only imagine what might have influenced the decision to use a set method to be learned for some people. This points to the Buddhist concept of skilful means — a very fluid approach to the eliciting of wisdom or inherent buddhanature — Buddha reportedly had 84,000 methods of pointing at and eliciting experience of the truth of reality.

What matters is not that the student matches with an offered template or produces a technique accurately. What matters is that they experience the desired result — ultimately awakening. The skill of the teacher is not in conveying or explaining awakening or instructing people in a set of rules to follow that led to that end, but in being observant and responsive enough to find the right way for each individual student to awake. These ways, in the history of Buddhism, have been idiosyncratic to say the least.

The precept of humbleness seems beautifully expressed here. When Usui was asked to pass healing techniques to Imperial officers in the army in 1923, who were interested in practical physical healing rather than entering a path of self-healing or spiritual development, he was not worried about preserving the purity of his fluid, organic, intuitive system in all its deep integrity. Instead he happily transmitted, through one of his leading students, a system involving symbols to create a short cut for the officers to use the aspect of his system they required – physical healing – quickly and effectively.

Usui did not, in fact, put particular emphasis on healing others at all - it was an effect not the purpose of practice. Likewise, particular hand positions may have been taught to some students but certainly not to all, and Usui's own healing practice was intuitive. Once the state has been achieved in which energy may flow unimpeded and merge with intention, the person who places their hands on another will be

50

instinctively drawn to put their hands where they are needed. All they need to do is merge with the energy and not get in the way with ego or interpretative thoughts of any kind, whether judging the person's condition or their own healing skills. Thinking about what you should be doing, or doing what you have been taught you should be doing regardless of the reality under your hands is only going to impede the healing — the state of energised wholeness for both treater and treatee — and ultimately everyone.

The system, which included intensifying meditation practice and study of the Lotus, Heart and Diamond Sutras which were fundamental to Tendai Buddhism and to Mahayana Buddhism in general (including Tibetan and Zen traditions), was an open ended one, it was never finished. The journey was lifelong, and certification did not apply.

Making this journey into a thing which can be bought and sold, transferred to others by means of a procedure, seems to me extremely unethical as well as ineffective. Of course it can't actually be manipulated into a thing, but it can be treated as if it were, and this treatment of 'it' and the people who enter the system of getting it (as people who have to learn to acquire something they do not already have from others who own the knowledge and are more powerful) desecrates the spirit of the original system. The original system is an expression of

ENERGY, INTUITION AND INTENTION.

Energy, just to recap, is what everything actually is, expressed in different forms in the relative world, as Buddhist language names it, 'the world of the ten thousand things'. Intuition is access to what and how everything is, as it's happening in one person, at one moment. Intention is that person attending to some part of what arises from the intuition, with their force and commitment. Whether this is an exercise of their free will or not is a separate question, I'm not sure in practice that it matters, maybe only for the practice of philosophy.

If you're working intuitively, then, you're working with what might be called the unconscious or subconscious mind, or the Tao. I find that this is best explicated, on a human level, by the work of the philosopher and therapist Eugene Gendlin.

Gendlin's Process Model

According to Gendlin's Process Model, the principle 'interaction first' is the basic principle.

It states that interaction is the basic primary force of the universe, hence it is the precursor to separate entities. Any entity you can think about or experience, including yourself, is a pattern derived from the original vast multiplicity of interactions. These interactions keep going throughout time, inter-affecting, becoming blocked, moving forward again, changed by all the other processes they have touched along the way, as some parts die and continue differently in the mix. Gendlin calls this the unseparated multiplicity, or the implicit intricacy, because any part you may separate out now to experience or think about contains all the previous processes implicit within it. You wouldn't be here to consider what the weather will be like tomorrow if it were not for the big bang, so all the chemical components present at that time are implicitly alive in your decision whether or not to take an umbrella to work.

The entirety of this information is not only extraneous, unnecessary for our purposes, but it would get in the way of doing anything — never mind the sheer impossibility of grasping even a miniscule proportion of it at any one time.

The way people generally function is according to what Gendlin calls the Unit Model. We lift elements out of the implicit intricacy and treat them as if they were separate units in order to manipulate them. This is indispensable for all kinds of mathematical, technological and psychological purposes. The unit model is no lesser than the implicit intricacy from which it is derived, it is indispensable in order for human life to be maintained, nowadays, as we live in larger societies, but it isn't appropriate for all areas of life.

Healing (maintaining free flow, a dynamic balance and oneness within a single organism, relationship, or larger organism such as a society or species) and use of life energy for creative purposes, spontaneous speech, dance, music, art, or any kind of improvisational response, are aspects of life which require the implicit intricacy to be drawn upon and lived. This is the way nature works, the Tao or the system in its entirety, going beyond what can be explained.

But we've already determined that being in touch with all of this implicit intricacy at one time (making it the explicit intricacy!) would be impossible and undesirable. So how to decide which aspect needs attention? You could gather information and use it to devise systems to work out which aspect should need attention, and see if the truth of the matter at any given moment as you perceive it matches up to that system. Or you could go the way of nature, using your intuition and paying attention in a certain way which enables what's relevant to a particular situation (a unique crossing of processes in space and time) to naturally arise. Gendlin operationalised this particular way of paying attention, calling it focusing. But before it was named and rendered into a technique for use when needed, focusing was just the way of natural life, living complex situations and sensing the next appropriate step, whether you're bird building a nest or a person improvising a dance or having a conversation. It still is.

Reiki has also been operationalised into a system, in fact a few different variants, lineages and cultures qualify in a similar way as their own systems. These are unit model ways of indicating the way to the actual source, the thing itself, energy passing through the hands (or eyes or breath, maybe the whole electro-magnetic field of a body) bringing a heightened aliveness and healing in its wake. Healing here could be defined as the next step, the next element which needs to shift, to produce better energy flow, to more ease, less suffering.

So when I write about Reiki from the roots, I'm not primarily concerned with being authentic and faithful to the original form in which Reiki was taught, as if this were of value in itself. I'm concerned with remaining faithful to the original source of the chi, rather than being distracted by the human unit model forms and all the opportunities they offer in which to match up or not match up with a concept, or to make new concepts and generalisations.

This model of engagement suits some people's natures and is very authentic to them, they're good at it, so this is a good thing for the world.

What I happen to be good at, though, what suits my nature, is refusing to be caught in the systems and always remaining in touch with the twisting thread of living life process and energy within it.

In Taoist terms, the energy, the Tao, while a primordial source beyond and encompassing everything we know and don't know, is also always present in our small, present moment human experience, forced into the shapes of the historical and cultural forms that have been imposed throughout human history, twisting from yin to yang and back again.

The Four Layers

The Reiki system adds an extra layer to the picture, which can be understood as four specific forms of the emptiness, or the Tao. There are four symbols, derived from the four kotodama: Focus, Harmony, (yin and yang, earth and sky) then Connection (a mental state, which occurs when the yin and yang join within the person) and finally Empowerment, the spiritual key to illumination. I will go into detail about these four layers in Chapter Five.

For our purposes here, the four layers cut through the binary system of yin and yang, first by adding awareness of oneness and connection itself, in a kind of third space, which can palpably be felt and worked with as a part of your experience, and then through the empowerment, illumination, which happens in another kind of space, not a form of energy in itself, but a way of experiencing pure light, a way of conceptualising and sensing what is beyond energy and the matter of experience.

Reiki from the roots to me is a way of living from and with the chi on all levels and all the intersections where they meet, and a way of living ethically, also on every level, from the everyday to the absolute, according to the precepts. The system was born from the idiosyncratic experience of one individual, Usui, who decided to cultivate the roots, the source of chi in himself in all the ways that presented them to him. His way will not be exactly my way or your way, but his example can be taken as yours, and his experience can be used to give you an incredible boost, living as it does now in your DNA, and expressed in ever-evolving cultural forms, including you, asking for your participation.

My part in its evolution is to sound the call to always remain close to what is actually happening, and not to what should be or could be happening or what we think rationally is happening or feel emotionally is happening. All these are elements of experience, but none of them should dominate.

Direct experience

Direct experience of the chi leads to unique intuitive actions, and at the same time strengthens the base. The base is made by commitment and intention, by returning endlessly to the breath, to the circuits of energy, to the chanting and to the internally spoken intention statements themselves, which are a crucial element in the power of Reiki, although easy to overlook.

When you start Reiki, you should say, internally or aloud, 'I am starting Reiki now'. You're making a declaration that has all the power associated with affirmations, and it works on your unconscious mind, which is no more nor less than the Tao itself. You're demarcating a sphere of action, and every time you draw this boundary, make this container in which to allow the chi to move in its own way, you're strengthening the habit, the form. The chi flocks and gathers to it, the practice becomes stronger, more energy can be held in the container, and more healing and nourishment and awakening may be experienced and done. When the statement is made strongly and firmly, it enables the passive, undirected aspect of the energy to be free and articulate.

Reiki is about holding a strong container, formed with ethics and intention, and then standing back entirely to allow the world to work as it does without your blockage and interference, to allow the chi to come through you as required. The intention of the Reiki master giving reiju empowerments is for 'what is needed' to occur, no more no less, with no personal interference or diagnosis from the master themselves regarding what they think the person may need, and without needing to believe or disbelieve the person's own interpretations or diagnoses either. The truth always encompasses both and goes well beyond.

The power of intention is in a sense a paradox, you're such a fleeting ephemeral part of the universe, yet it's enough to experiment or play with the power of intention and declaration for it to become abundantly clear that all you need to do is drop resistance and simply state how things are for your subconscious to listen. And your subconscious is not separate from the Tao, the emptiness, the source of energy. It doesn't come from anywhere else.

In this way people can, using intention, send healing energy to people wherever they are in the world, with or without any particular movements or rituals, and without any understanding of quantum entanglement. You can send chi to yourself, or rather awareness of a specific form of chi, at some point in the future, with or without using visualising techniques. You can 'order' Reiki to be experienced by a recipient at a particular time, and then forget all about it. They may or may not know the energy will be sent. It will happen, not by ritual, although rituals can strengthen the container. It happens by intent, by declaration. This intent, when we use Reiki, always includes the tenet that the recipient receives what is needed. Hence it isn't personally invasive.

This is not the case when using other energy systems, in which energy may be sent to others which is unwanted or which is experienced as heavy, inappropriate, or may even impede healing by cluttering up the recipients' system. This can happen particularly, in my experience, when large helpings of energy of lower density, say the Cho Ku Rei earthly chi, are sent to someone who's suffering on a much more subtle level and who, through energy practices or simple affinity is open to high frequencies. What we might call Western Reiki has rules prohibiting sending Reiki to people without their consent.

In the world of the ten thousand things, the world of selves and others, of boundaries and rights, quite simply in the relative world you and I live in, this makes perfect sense. But when I say that consent isn't necessary when using Reiki properly, this isn't to say that Reiki and its practitioners are immune to error or superior.

There are two reasons. Firstly, plugging into and stating the intention for the energy to be used as the other person needs it is truly powerful, and includes the option for the person to refuse it, or feel nothing if this is what they request.

Secondly and most essentially, if you're living with constant empowerments (energy work, meditations, chanting) bathing in Reiki, and living according to the precepts that keep your mind clear and your container strong, good luck with not sending reiki to anyone who crosses your mind, on a daily basis! You can't help but do so because on an absolute level, we're all one. Not a monolithic mass, but a mass of inseparable living interconnections made out of the same energy yet with many faces, and the more you cultivate awareness of this, the less you will block it and the more your life will be a free, organic flow of sending Reiki all around you, to the food you eat, the elements, the world, the people you see on the internet, or speak to in real life. Explicit, organised consent holds only on the relative level. On the deeper level there is the free will to block, to say no, and that can't be overridden. But there is no need for someone who is open to Reiki to be informed of planned time and space co-ordinates. It will be spontaneous, between people who care about each other or who think about each other. It would be absurd to stop it. You cannot stop love.

CHAPTER FOUR

REIJU EMPOWERMENTS, REIKI ENERGY PRACTICES

Usui performed empowerments, known as reiju, for his students, often by intention only, for the good of and according to the need of the recipient. This is sometimes translated as the giving of the five blessings, or five powers, in accord with Tendai Buddhism.

The five powers allow the student to develop fundamental qualities from which the Buddhist Way is cultivated:

1. The Power of Faith (Confidence)

2. The Power of Zeal (Energy, Effort)

3. The Power of Mindfulness

4. The Power of Meditation

5. The Power of Wisdom' (King, 2005, p.142)

These powers go far beyond attuning a student to a particular form of energy in order to heal self or others. The five powers may or may not be transferred through the placing of hands. What is certain is that the one bestowing the blessing must have 'got out of the way' to a great extent, through their own cultivation of the five powers. These powers aren't ends in themselves, or states which might be attained. They're ways of clearing the clutter from the natural way of things.

Faith clears doubt, or the worry pointed to in the first precept. Zeal clears anger, putting that assertive energy to good use, mindfulness also keeps you safe from worry and other mental storylines, as you observe them and keep returning to the breath and the sensations of the present moment. Mental storylines such as worrying are pretty much always vain attempts to control the past or the future. Mindfulness meditation is a way of honing the skill of not dwelling too long in such storylines, learning to move your attention back to base, not allowing yourself to identify with the storyline, believe it, become submerged in it or addicted to it.

Once mindfulness has put you in charge of your own attention and the space in your mind is constantly in the process of being cleared, a stillness arises, a calm strength, a space and energy for other forms of meditation. And from meditation, wisdom naturally arises. Wisdom isn't a set of facts to be acquired but a quality arising from being with bodily life, mental, emotional and physical, as it is, in a skilful way, using different ways of accessing and playing with the energy you're made of to help you remove the weight of obstructions, pains and traumas caused by your own ignorance, leading you to act, for example, as if your needs were contrary to those of others.

Hara, Tantien Exercises

Usui paid a great deal of attention to the hara (abdomen area) otherwise known as the lower tantien, the centre of power within the body, to be found two fingers breadths below the navel and a couple of centimetres into the body. According to the Taoist system there are three main energy centres in the body, one in the abdomen, one in the chest, the heart region, and one in the head. Keeping the centre of gravity in the lower tantien is vital for centring, grounding, balance and access to the raw source power needed in order to do anything. It keeps you from becoming lost in thoughts and feelings and enables you to concentrate, from a safe base. Awareness, energy, breath, light can all be collected here. If your life feels scattered, out of control, or unsatisfactory in any way, this can be the single most helpful thing.

Taoist Practices

My approach to Taoist practices is spontaneous and intuitive and the ones which have become a natural part of my life, increasing the flow of energy through my hands and the strength available for others, untainted by any of my own content, involve placing my awareness into the back of my body, rather than the front, as taught to me by Taoist master teacher Stephen Russell. It's hard to put into words what a revelation this simple, concrete practice has been to me, and it's a tiny, invisible shift that can be performed at any time.

Making the backwards shift

You shift your energy into your back, as if you had a side seam running down your body, and all your weight were in the back half, leaving the front half free. Power, centredness, perspective, intention all become freely available, unhooked from the mental and sense distractions that go on in the front of your brain and in front of your eyes.

Shifting backwards, and then flowing and flying backwards are the strongest of all the practices I've learned from the Taoist system, moving counter to the mad stressful dash forwards towards death that I used to engage in for most of my waking hours. Timelessness, raw power and all the information lying within the subconscious, may be physically felt and are there to draw upon once you make that simple psycho-physical move with your energy. Try it. Lean back against the back wall of your skull, as if it were a cave and rest. Don't get involved.

Other practices which had strong physical effects on my energy flow (and to be honest I couldn't keep up the consistency or find the motivation to carry on with any other kind) involved sending energy around the microcosmic orbit which runs up the back of the spine and down the front of the body in a loop, meeting at the perineum. This microcosmic orbit also appears in Reiki exercises and attunements, as does the importance of keeping a closed loop of energy in order to intensify its power for specific use. The microcosmic orbit involves the two main energy channels according to the Chinese medicine system, the Governor channel up the back of the spine, providing raw yang power, and the channel down the front providing yin grace.

One of the first clients who came to me became spontaneously attuned to Reiki after one session, and then practically begged me to give her the formal attunement. With my natural antipathy to matching one thing to another and seeing this as some kind of an achievement, I gave her the reiju empowerment, a simple and direct full body energy experience for both of us, with no intervening symbols or complicated procedures to distract my attention in any way, shape or form from the matter in hand — forging a new connection path as powerfully and directly as possible.

This sense of forging a direct path through intention, and harnessing the primordial power of the universe, is what lies at the root of Reiki for me, and it's a sad indication of the state of affairs when this sounds like something lofty or abstract or overblown or ridiculous in normal cultural parlance. The amount of attention, intention and faith we place in the world of our constructs is amazing — we put so much energy into our systems of languages, technologies, countries, while completely ignoring the fact that we are born, and die, on a big rock spinning in unimaginably vast space among millions of other stars and planets and have no idea what happens before birth or after death, let alone why any of it happens. The Unit Model we've constructed is incredible and worthy of effort and attention, but not to the point at which the implicit intricacy containing everything is colonised out of the narrative completely, appearing as something secondary rather than prior and fundamental. Far from being a luxury, supplying extra good feelings on top of 'real life', doing Reiki is paying attention to your own participation in real life — the stuff it's actually composed of. It's the versions of reality which pay no attention to energy which are like communal hallucinations, efficient co-manifestations, working on agreed and oft-declared principles about how the world is. These manifestations are ultimately based in intention and committed action, to make it the way we say it is.

So you can also place all that intention and action-potential into how it really is — and from that point of non-denial, no longer wasting energy in pushing upstream, create a strong structure simply by holding that awareness of the nature of things – and within a strong structure, the energy flows by itself to heal, energise, bring thoughts, feelings, intuitions, whatever is needed - unimpeded and as powerfully as possible given the particular conditions.

The energy, as previously mentioned, comes in two main flavours, two forms, earth and sky or yin and yang, and there are two further energy states which form parts of the Reiki system. In the next chapter, I'll take them one by one and go into them in a bit more depth.

CHAPTER FIVE

KOTODAMA – ENERGIES/INTENTIONS

The kotodama are central to the Reiki eco-system. Chanting produces different frequencies directly in the body of the practitioner, and out into the air, or rather the frequencies you produce resonate with the frequencies already out there.

CHO KU REI

watch and learn

from the raindrops

hollowing the stone

discard the thought

of a difficult task

(05 Occasional thought, Emporer Meiju, Waka poem, my translation (from Rivard, R 2007).

The first word-spirit, energy aspect, called into being by a Shinto mantra, is CHO KU REI – the energy of earth.

This is chi in its densest physical form. The symbol for this kind of energy is known in some Reiki circles as the power symbol, use of which cranks up the force, adds a kind of acceleration to whatever you're doing. This earth energy is of a dense, material, fundamental, grounding, low frequency. It is about focus, and physical healing.

Physical energy is, obviously, felt in a palpable way. When I call upon this energy — after becoming familiar with it through chanting — or rather when I concentrate on it, bracketing all other experiences I'm having at the same time, I feel density, earth and fire. It's physically very hot in the hands. The energy has a lower vibration — this isn't a moral judgement, it just means a literally slower vibration. In sound terms it's a lower note. A very low note is in a sense more powerful than a higher one, there's more of it, it has a massive resonance and presence, while on the other hand it could be said that a very high note is more piercing and cuts through more clearly. At the end of the day the volume of power is equal but the forms are different, they are ultimately inseparable, and all aspects are equally needed.

Throughout my life I've had a tendency to want to skip the earth energy and get straight to what I thought of as the more interesting bits — the heaven, the spirit, the intangible and mysterious and what I defined as more powerful.

It took a while, maybe the experience of pregnancy and birth were crucial, for me to realise that without a body, there is simply no experience at all. Without roots there's no tree. Without the rest of the bird, the wings cannot function.

More, there's a wealth, an absurd density of richness of experience, power and pleasure in the realm of the body, nature, matter (and no difference in essence between body, nature and matter).

In a sense it's the starting point.

In another sense it's the sticking point. Much subtle experience can be short circuited by chronic pain or illness.

Without the earth chi there's nothing else, no human experience, no animal experience, no plant experience. Without the body, the earth, there's no arena, without the container, no contents.

The earth, the animals, nature, cycles, all have the dense energy of the binary, dark and light. This energy feels elemental, fire, earth, air, water, it's sensual, you can touch it, it's sexual, where organic life comes from, embodied. It throbs, pulsates with blood, circulation. Dense with muscles, nerves, flesh. It exists as green, brown, trees, earth, mulch and compost enabling plants to grow, moisture, moss, rest.

Cho ku rei is used, in Reiki, to heal on the physical level. It is most natural to heal like with like, rather than causing conflict between levels, by, say, trying to heal a basic problem with an abstract solution, earth with heaven.

This is the kind of chi movement in the lower tantien which is intensified in the practice or cultivation of internal alchemy. The animal drive, the life force on its most basic level, raw power, earthy and sexual, is drawn from the perineum to the belly, or lower tantien (or hara) where it turns into will.

The will to heal on the level of matter, of what our bodies are made of, with all the interconnections and consequences of that, happens with the cho ku rei. Or, cho ku rei is one way of encapsulating that.

SEI I KI

The Heaven (sky)

early green

clears away

the great sky

large and broad

along with my own heart

(02 'Ten' The Heaven, sky. Emporer Meiju, Waka poem, my translation from Rivard, R 2007).

66

The second energy to be experienced and bathed in is heavenly energy, more delicate and of higher, faster frequency. It works on mental and emotional planes, activating release and balance.

This is the energy that streams from heaven, light in frequency, and also associated with or experienced as physical light. It's a higher frequency and note. It's the energy of thoughts and feelings, ideas, concepts, dreams and human experience in the aspect in which it feels unhooked from the body.

When this energy appears in Reiki it heals, in the sense of soothing overactive thoughts and feelings, or activating them in someone who feels overwhelmed or dragged down by the density of physical life.

This could be interpreted as an inbetween stage, a uniquely human one, between organic matter/physical life and the spiritual.

It's the kind of chi movement, when you practice internal alchemy, that goes from the belly, the lower centre of chi containment and cultivation, up to the heart, where pure will transforms into love.

The heart centre is the centre not only of warm fuzziness, but of wisdom. With scientific discoveries about the extent of the electro-magnetic field of the heart and the importance of heart coherence, this has become more clearly acknowledged recently. The heart centre is busy processing energy. Its activities are less obviously visible. Actions often seem to come from the lower power centre. These actions may be, though, infused with love. This is qualitatively different from an addition, sweetener, or some special sauce poured over your activities from on high. Love is the infusion of chi which constitutes the action.

It's implicit in the action. Actually almost everything that makes up an action is implicit. Everything else is just what we

can see. All the mass of interconnections making it possible —
what Gendlin calls the 'implicit intricacy' — are infinite as far
as anyone can know. Without needing to make explicit forms,
and without wasting energy trying, the heart can process more
of this complexity than the mind.

Love moves faster than the speed of thought. Maybe love
moves faster than the speed of light. It moves like instinct
moves, before we know why.

HO A ZE HO NE

> the autumn moon
>
> does not change
>
> for such a long time
>
> the deceased
>
> from this world
>
> are increasing

(o1 'Tsuki' The moon. Emporer Meiju, Waka poem, my translation from
Rivard, R, 2007).

This is the connection kotodama. It isn't an energy to be
channelled, experienced, bathed in or given to others. It's a
state of mind that arises during meditation and energy
practices, a state of the recognition of oneness. The
connection frequency, or intention — or intention frequency,
floods the mind — there may be a specific sensation. The
connection spirit causes the conditions for distance healing to
occur, and also makes connections alive and felt within the
systems of individual people, enabling their heads and hearts,
thoughts and emotions to work as one rather than hold
themselves tensely apart due to some mental storyline.

This is not an energy as such but a state evoked, created or remembered, in the person who is calling upon and transmitting Reiki. In this state, the earthly and the heavenly energies are one – the feel of the state for me is like being lifted up a gear, released, it feels both light and powerful, the density and texture of the earth and the translucent form of the heavens are transmuted, both somehow present in a state of complete concentration, which feels like a tremendous relief.

There's no need to hold everything separate and apart.

There is no linearity at all.

Form is emptiness and emptiness is form, and the bodily experience of this, through calling on that state with full awareness of the energies involved, goes far beyond the conceptual head-game of it.

This connection, or co-existence state is always used for distance healing, and the absolute presence of the person on the receiving end, juxtaposed with their relative absence, feels shockingly appropriate, a giving up of the pretence of separation from them, the difference between giver and receiver, our being divided by space and time. This feels like the dimension of truth. It feels like home. I place my hands on someone directly, wherever they are.

It feels like a relief, and relief is always a sign of the real, rather than the illusion.

This is what happens in the internal alchemy process when you pull the chi upwards from the heart to the head, then up above it, where love transforms into pure consciousness.

This state is the 'material' from which the immortal spirit body is formed. Only love can merge with wisdom to make real power — by real I mean not just what can be seen.

AI I KO YO

This kotodama expresses the light of total illumination, it's the master key. More than a mental state, it's the state of awakening, the state expressed by Buddhist sutras as luminosity. It is used by Reiki masters to empower others to perform empowerments to others. It has the highest vibration of all and is used in healing on a soul level, explicitly reaching the person's entire system, encompassing and exceeding the physical, mental and emotional, and going beyond even the sense of oneness.

This state of illumination is absolute light, a vibration so fast and high that it's beyond energy as we conceptualise it. All-encompassing, it forms a note that can't actually be heard by the human ear, but can be felt. It is clearly beyond all elements of human experience, yet it plays within the instrument of the body.

This is the master key, which unlocks what is beyond language, earth, sky, physical, mental, emotional and spiritual awareness. It has an unlocking and a cutting quality — reaching right through to what is beyond. It lasers in on the stuck points of suffering which are not strictly physical, mental, emotional or spiritual. It lasers in on the stuck points in some deeper place you might call the soul.

This lifts the whole system and infuses it with the unsayable. It's the essence of love, joy, compassion, the previously discussed energies and the state of oneness intrinsic and implicit within it. This is the kotodama or symbol to use with people who are locked into deep self-hatred or deep patterns of addiction or trauma which go beyond 'themselves', maybe ancestral pains, or spiritual dis-ease.

The frequency of the key goes on, unlocking and illuminating.

This kotodama expresses the essence of Mahayana Buddhism, a state of illumination which is said to be both luminous and groundless. A state, from the psychological point of view, of complete insecurity and complete security — the only kind there is, because it remains unchanging in a world characterised by constant change. Beyond the state of connection and as-it-is-ness of Ho a Ze Ho Ne, it's best expressed as in the Heart Sutra. simply by the word 'beyond'!

The sutra ends 'gate gate paragate parasamgate bodhi svaha!' 'gone, gone, gone beyond, gone completely beyond — ' and then an exclamation of welcome and praise as the person reaches the shore at which all shores disappear.

The texture, the full-on visceral experience of wisdom and compassion at the same time, almost forcibly clears the mind, flushing out all thinking and feelings that are sources of suffering.

The way in which these four word-spirits encapsulate different aspects of reality — not in a solid structure that different activities should conform to, but in a constant dance, renders the whole constellation a beautiful and effective one to work/dance within.

CHAPTER SIX

POWER, RECEPTIVITY, LOVE

The cultivation and transmission of Reiki can be learnt only through doing — and it isn't the reproduction of particular techniques which produces results, it's not a technological procedure, but a living one, which comes about through intention, and inner movements of attention.

The ability to cultivate and transmit reiki is passed on not by one person placing 'something' inside another, but by someone transmitting the chi in a manner so clear, strong and unified that the person with the intention to receive can resonate clearly with it, and all salient differences between the giver and receiver collapse. This is how Usui gave empowerments simply by looking at people. It wasn't because he himself possessed some kind of special individual magic, it was because he was able to be in a state of resonance with the chi and the source of the chi, which comes before its separation into forms. He was not running any interference on it in those moments.

The definition of activity can be widened. By 'just' looking at someone you're doing a lot — there are millions — literally millions — of interconnected processes happening during that moment, that person, that intentional activity/set-up of theirs, that gaze. And these processes/activities can be picked up by the one 'being looked at'. Language fails once more. It isn't one person picking something up from another, rather that the looking is participated in, or rather a common participation starts up. This is how reiju empowerments work.

The receptive mode is not about being ready to allow any particular thing to happen or enter, it's about making yourself open and unobstructed so you can take part in activities which would not be possible in habitual, more closed down modes of functioning.

Reiki in general is all about the receptive mode. Being in this mode is healing in itself, it gives the healing activities implicit in our bodies/mental/emotional systems space and a chance to work.

Being in receptive mode is the crucial step in both giving and receiving Reiki empowerments and Reiki treatments. It's what makes them work. The power of Reiki is the consistent way in which it points to this receptive state at all times, stressing that the practitioner needs to stand aside, rather than diagnose or direct the flow in any way.

Within the receptive state there is complete trust, a kind of trust without object, just in what is so completely happening. There's no need for belief or faith as such because there's direct experience of the chi flowing through. If you feel it isn't flowing, that means there's still mental activity going on, distracting your attention. The flow of chi is basic, fundamental. As soon as distractions are removed (and pretty much all mental, physical and emotional activity works as a distraction from the sheer, contentless flow itself), the flow will be sensed (to varying extents depending on the person, and after Reiki empowerments or attunements, this becomes easier). When concentration and focus is applied, that flow can be used for any purpose.

Empowerments and attunements are the methods specific to Reiki of accessing, or entering, this kind of concentration and focus. They are extra powerful due to the specific way they cross the (ultimately artificial) boundaries between one person and another. They activate within the Reiki master doing the empowerment or attunement and in the receiver too, forming yet another lesson on the necessity of being in the receptive state, and proof of your efficacy when you do.

Everything just works better. This is what healing is about really. It's not necessarily about striding in to immediately change the large scale conditions in the body, but it's always about enabling different processes to work better within those conditions. What is a 'large scale' condition is also a relative matter. At the end of the day, pain and death are parts of the human condition, death can't be healed, and the 'balance' within the system or organism that you might catch when you call yourself or a condition 'healed' is fleeting in the larger scale of things.

However you also have influence on your experience of pain and death at every step of the way, and while there may be entry points everywhere — you might for instance use mental techniques — the most powerful way, cutting right to the chase, is by plugging straight into the power source itself, what you might call the Tao, for want of a better word — the pure energy source both behind and within everything that lives (and, spookily, apparently in everything that doesn't, but never mind that for now).

Being in receptive mode is also a way of living.

In this mode, you're receptive to the next step.

Next step healing

Healing isn't a one-off, all-encompassing action. There's no static state of balance to be achieved, there's no perfect health. There is, always, though a small shift that can be made somewhere in the direction of freedom or ease.

A shift in one place can't help but affect everything to some degree. The human experience is not made up of discrete entities. Once again we're looking at relative and absolute levels, at how the life force/energy can be impeded, but not destroyed. There are certainly single events that can kill you as the temporarily whole human being you are. But there isn't one single event that can bring every part of you into a state of optimum functioning.

Also, the slightest shift of attention can't fail to have an effect on more than you can know. More than you know is implicit in everything you touch, think about, or love. This is the implicit intricacy, the Tao. Just treating yourself, and others, with awareness that this is the case, rather than concentrating on an underlyingly competitive model of one 'thing' at the expense of 'others' is intrinsically healing.

Healing is attention-energy given to the wholeness of things.

When you pay this attention — a next step always appears.

There might be a fear of this not happening, a fear that if you pay attention to the fact that everything is implicitly present, then you will somehow slide off into everything, become everywhere and nowhere, indistinct, non-specific, spaced out, incapable of action.

If you're paying attention, really bringing presence to a pain, a thought, a feeling, the opposite is true.

This attention, presence, brings the chi. The chi brings more attention and presence. The more attention you're using, the more present you are, the more receptive you are to the next step. The next tiny, specific constellation of everything forms in the moment and the body that you are.

Something is released — the tension created by holding things separately, by trying to control reality, push a single storyline, be actively making something up and doing it by force.

In receptivity, all the chi is released for use. And given all the myriad causes and conditions at play, there's only really one small channel of possibility through which it can flow. Place your attention on just this place, this moment, and see.

There's a sigh of relief, there's a movement forward, there's a second in which nothing feels out of balance. There's an agreement with how things are, an accord. There's a moment free of suffering and it may even be a moment free of physical pain. This is healing.

You can't expect it to last forever, because nothing does. Accepting this fact, not just rationally, but actually, emotionally, spiritually, with all the chi that's flowing through you, and your own free will, is healing.

So concentrating on being a receptive channel for Reiki, without your own contents for that time in which you are intentionally enabling the flow to come through you, creates instances of healing, a flow of healing, and also brings actions, insights, feelings and changes on any level you turn your attention to. This goes for the recipient of the Reiki and also for the 'giver'.

A moment of receptive presence and unblocked flow (which starts with an intention to do a Reiki session) has no boundaries unless they're consciously erected by the recipient. It will work anyhow and anywhere, it works everywhere.

This has been tried and tested, in my experience and that of many others. An interesting question arises from it. All you have to do is remove the boundaries. Could this receptive presence and unblocked flow, mysteriously, intrinsically, experienced as love, extend into the whole world — were the illusive boundaries of the separate 'things' not put up? Would the whole abusive and exploitative set of systems based on accumulating 'things' and owning more and more of them then collapse?

Is there a way the natural boundaries between the forms which the world works on could be held in a lighter way, so they do not obstruct the flow but dance with it?

The isness of form is emptiness, and emptiness is form. Reiki is the very isness of the forms, the energy which can't be 'had'. The healing can't be individualised, and we shouldn't try. In creating the proper conditions for the Reiki to flow, both form and emptiness, giver and receiver, subject and object, disappear. That is precisely, and only, what is important. The practice of Reiki is not an escape, unless we erect a boundary between 'this experience of mine' and 'everyday life' or 'this experience of mine' and 'other people'.

To truly heal, you can ask 'where has a boundary been erected in a way that's hurting the person, where is power, the power to make and enforce boundaries, to have and possess things, in the realm of the relative, the world of the ten thousand things, being used badly?

You have the energy to tackle that. In these times, this is exactly what Reiki is for. To challenge the relative forms of power and making 'things', and the conflict between them, and to charge yourself up for this, as the conflict and the sense of lostness and trauma become more intense under the pressure of events.

It's too late in the day for awakening for the sake of awakening — which might have been possible within a fundamentally stable, if unjust, system. The system now is, as it always was, in a fluid dynamic balance, but it's more unstable than ever before, because the limits of tolerance are being reached, the planet's tolerance for human life and human tolerance for each other.

Consciously accessing and engaging with the chi-element of all events and people, means giving up the death-grip of the active mode alone, which literally exhausts and sucks the life out of everything. It means allowing the receptive power of love to flow — and it's really a matter of urgency right now. The power can then be used for all the actions that are needed. It will also show you what they are.

Focus.

You can feel it. It's in the palm of your hand.

BIBLIOGRAPHY

Barefoot Doctor, Russell, S. 2017. Superhealing: Wayward Publications

Barefoot Doctor, Russell, S. 2017. Driving With Your Eyes Closed: Wayward Publications

Gendlin, E. 1997. A Process Model. The Focusing Institute.

Heart Sutra, trans. Hsuan-Tsang, n.d.

King, Taggart, 1998-2005 Reiki Master/Teacher Course Manual: Shinpiden: Reiki Evolution

Lubeck, W. 1995 The Complete Reiki Handbook: Lotus Light:Shangri-La

Luczaj, S. 2015. 'Felt Senses of Self and No-Self' PhD thesis, UEA

Luczaj S. 2020. 'Focusing is not a thing' in Senses of Focusing, ed. Moore, J and Krypriotakis, N. Eurasia Publications: Athens forthcoming publication

Lao Tsu. 1972. Tao Te Ching. Translated by Feng, G. F. and English, J. London: Wildwood House Ltd.

Rivard, Richard R. (1999, 2000, 2007) Reiki Ryoho Hikkei 2 @Universal Copyright

Also by Sarah Luczaj

Creative Regeneration (2019)

CPSIA information can be obtained
at www.ICGtesting.com
Printed in the USA
LVHW021325210121
676969LV00007B/1008